Instant

File-Folder Games for Reading

by Marilyn Myers Burch

SCHOLASTIC

PROFESSIONAL BOOKS

New York • Toronto • London • Auckland • Sydney
Mexico City • New Delhi • Hong Kong • Buenos Aires

This book is dedicated to my husband David who continues to support me and my writing.

Acknowledgments

I'd like to thank the following people for all of the work they have put into this book to make it such an attractive and useful resource for teachers and students:

Danielle Blood and Linda Ward Beech, editors

Rusty Fletcher, artist

Jaime Lucero and Sydney Wright, graphic designers

Cover design by Jaime Lucero

Interior design by Sydney Wright

Cover and interior illustration by Rusty Fletcher

ISBN 0-439-13731-4

Contents

To the Teacher

Instant File-Folder Games for Reading offers an engaging and fun way to reinforce important reading and language arts skills. Just photocopy and color the game boards, glue them inside file folders, and you've got ten instant reading-center activities! The games are a snap to set up and store: Each game has a handy pocket on the front of the file folder in which to store the reproducible directions and game parts. Kids will have fun as they practice synonyms with Peas in a Pod, initial consonants with Bike Race, vocabulary skills with Word Hop, and much more.

Playing games is a great way to motivate children of all learning styles to build language arts skills. There are a variety of ways you can use these games to meet the needs of your students. Store the games in a reading center and encourage students to play before or after school, during free time, or when they have finished other tasks. You can also send games home for students to play with family members and friends. Use the Extending the Game suggestions to continue to build students' skills and interest.

How to Use This Book

Each game comes with an introductory page for the teacher that provides a suggestion for introducing the game, step-by-step directions for assembling the game, and activities to extend learning. Each game also includes several reproducible elements: a label for the file-folder tab; a pocket for the front of the file folder in which to store the game parts; directions for the students that explain how to play the game; an answer key; and a game board. Some games also include cards, playing pieces, and a spinner. To enhance the game board and playing pieces, you may wish to have students color them.

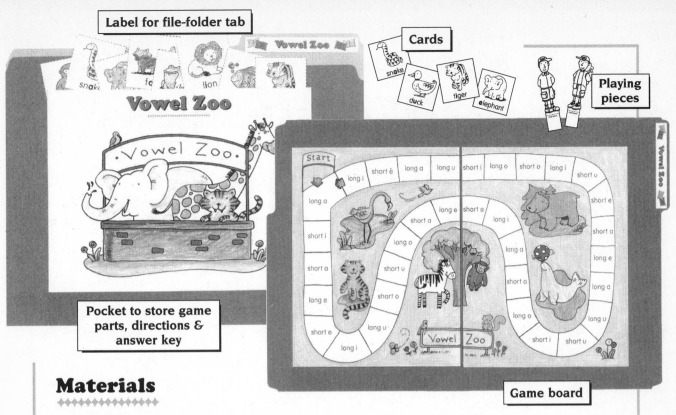

Label for file-folder tab

Cards

Playing pieces

Pocket to store game parts, directions & answer key

Game board

Materials

In addition to the reproducible game pages, you'll need the following:

* 10 file folders
* scissors
* paper fasteners
* tape
* playing pieces (such as chips, beans, or pennies)

* glue or rubber cement
* paper clips
* crayons or colored pencils

Tips

◆ Laminate the game parts to enhance sturdiness and durability.

◆ Conduct mini-lessons to review the skills required in each game.

◆ Model for students how to play each game.

◆ Use a different color for each game label.

◆ Give children suggestions on how to determine the order in which players take turns, such as rolling a die and taking turns in numerical order.

Storage Ideas

Keep the file-folder games in any of these places:

* reading resource center
* vertical file tray
* file box

* file cabinet
* bookshelf

Vowel Zoo

Skill: This game provides practice in recognizing long and short vowels.

Introduction

◆◆◆◆◆◆◆◆◆◆◆◆◆◆◆◆◆◆◆◆◆

Review long and short vowels with students. Show students the animal cards and encourage them to use the pictures to help them read the words.

◆◆◆◆◆◆◆◆◆◆◆◆◆◆◆◆◆◆◆◆ **Assembling the Game** ◆◆◆◆◆◆◆◆◆◆◆◆◆◆◆◆◆◆◆◆

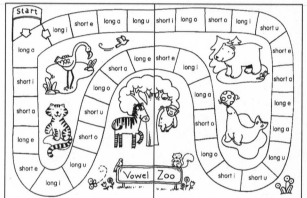

1. Duplicate and cut out the file-folder label and pocket on page 7. Glue the label onto the tab of the file folder. Tape the pocket on three sides to the outside front of the folder.

2. Duplicate and cut out the directions, answer key, and cards on pages 8–9. When the game is not in use, store these items in the pocket on the front of the folder.

3. Make several copies of the playing pieces below. Color each playing piece a different color. Fold the tabs so that the pieces stand up.

4. Duplicate, cut out, and glue or tape together the number cube on page 36.

5. Duplicate and cut out the game board on pages 10–11. Invite students to color the game board, and then glue it onto the inside of the folder.

Extending the Game

◆◆◆◆◆◆◆◆◆◆◆◆◆◆◆◆◆◆◆◆◆◆◆◆◆◆◆◆

◆ Use the game cards as flash cards. Have children read the word and tell whether the vowel in bold is long or short.

◆ Have students choose a long or short vowel. Invite them to list as many words as they can that include that vowel sound.

Vowel Zoo

Label and Pocket

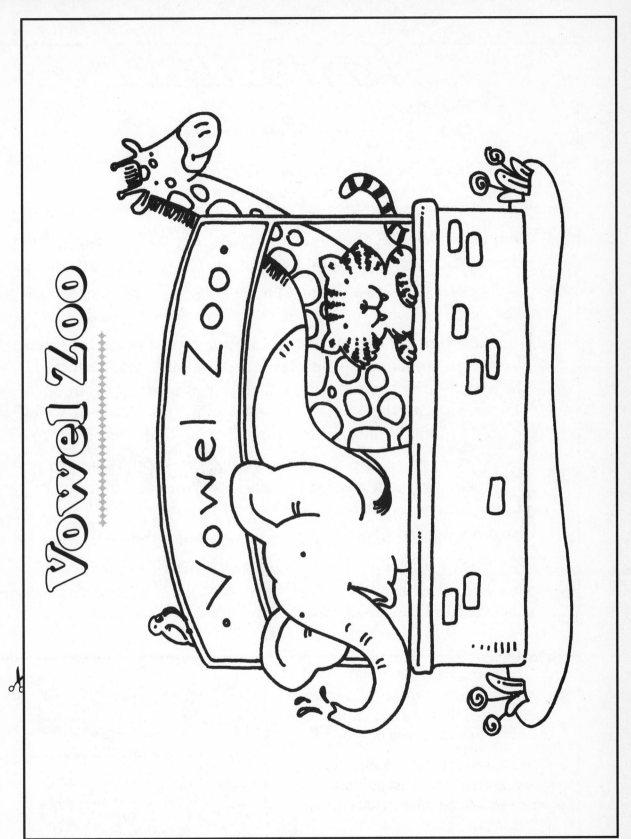

Vowel Zoo

Vowel Zoo

Vowel Zoo

Directions for Play
(for 2–4 Players)

One player shuffles the cards and deals five cards to each player. The remaining cards are not needed.

Each player chooses a playing piece. Players place their pieces on Start.

To take a turn, a player rolls the number cube and moves forward that number of spaces. The player reads aloud what is written in the space—for example, long e. The player looks at his or her cards for a word that contains that vowel sound. (Note: The vowel in bold letters on the card must match the vowel on the space.)

If the player has a card with a matching vowel sound, he or she places the card in a discard pile and the turn ends. If the player does not have a matching card, the turn ends.

Players continue to take turns, moving around the board. The first player to get rid of all his or her cards is the winner. (Note: Players can move around the game board as many times as necessary.)

Answer Key

long a: snake, whale
short a: yak, alligator

long e: zebra, seal
short e: elephant, penguin

long i: tiger, lion
short i: fish, chimp

long u: unicorn, porcupine
short u: duck, cub

long o: hippo, toad
short o: frog, fox

Vowel Zoo

Cards

sn**a**ke	wh**a**le	y**a**k	**a**lligator
z**e**bra	s**e**al	**e**lephant	p**e**nguin
t**i**ger	l**i**on	f**i**sh	ch**i**mp
unicorn	porc**u**pine	d**u**ck	c**u**b
hipp**o**	t**o**ad	fr**o**g	f**o**x

Vowel Zoo

Game Board

Start

long i

short e

long a

long u

long a

long e

short a

short i

long o

short a

short u

long e

short o

short e

long u

long i

Vowel

Trim off this strip and attach to page 11.

Vowel Zoo

Game Board

short i | long o | short o | long i | short u

short e | short e

long i | short a

long a | long e

short o | long a

long o | long u

Attach to page 10 here.

Zoo

short i | short u

Word Family Flowers

Skill: Children practice grouping words into word families.

Introduction

Review common word family endings with students.

Assembling the Game

1 Duplicate and cut out the file-folder label and pocket on page 13. Glue the label onto the tab of the file folder. Tape the pocket on three sides to the outside front of the folder.

2 Duplicate and cut out the directions, answer key, and cards on pages 14–15. When the game is not in use, store these items in the pocket on the front of the folder.

3 Duplicate and cut out game board sides 1 and 2 on pages 16–17. Invite students to color the game board, and then glue it onto the inside of the folder.

Extending the Game

◆ Use the game cards as flash cards. Have children read the word and identify its word family.

◆ Have students choose a word family. Invite them to list as many words in that word family as they can. Then challenge students to write or dictate a short story using the words on the list.

Word Family Flowers

Label and Pocket

Word Family Flowers

Word Family Flowers

Word Family Flowers

Directions for Play
(for 2 Players)

1 Each player chooses one side of the game board.

2 One player shuffles the cards and places them facedown in a stack.

3 The first player chooses the top card and reads the word. If the word belongs in one of the word families on his or her side of the board, the player places the card on a petal of that word family flower. If the card does not belong, the player places the card in a discard pile.

4 Players take turns. When there are no more cards in the stack, players shuffle and use the cards in the discard pile. The first player to fill all the petals on his or her side of the board wins.

Answer Key

Side 1:
-an: can, fan, man, pan
-ice: price, mice, dice
-ug: rug, mug, hug

Side 2:
-ing: king, sing, swing
-aw: saw, draw, straw
-ip: skip, ship, rip, drip

Word Family Flowers

Cards

can fan man pan

saw draw straw price

mice dice king sing

swing skip ship rip

drip rug mug hug

Word Family Flowers

-an

-ice

slice

-ug

bug

Trim off this strip and attach to page 17.

Word Family Flowers

Game Board Side 2

All Aboard!

Skill: Children practice reading words with blends and digraphs.

Introduction

Review the following blends and consonant digraphs that appear in the game. Invite children to think of words that begin with each blend and digraph.

Blends: *dr, fl*

Consonant digraphs: *ch, th*

✦✦✦✦✦✦✦✦✦✦✦✦✦✦✦✦✦✦ Assembling the Game ✦✦✦✦✦✦✦✦✦✦✦✦✦✦✦✦✦✦

1 Duplicate and cut out the file-folder label and pocket on page 19. Glue the label onto the tab of the file folder. Tape the pocket on three sides to the outside front of the folder.

2 Duplicate and cut out the directions, answer key, and cards on pages 20–21. When the game is not in use, store these items in the pocket on the front of the folder.

3 Make two copies of the game board on page 23. Invite students to color the game boards, and then glue them onto the inside of the folder, as shown.

4 Duplicate the spinner on page 22 and mount it on posterboard or laminate it. Unbend the end of a paper clip and use it to punch a hole in the center of the spinner. Place the round end of the paper clip over the hole and attach it with a brass fastener. Or spin the paper clip around a pencil tip, as shown.

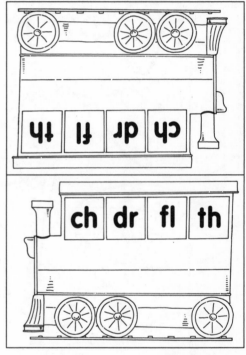

Extending the Game

✦ Make additional word cards that contain the blends and digraphs on the game board.

The Fast and Easy Way

Brass fastener

The Sturdy Way

All Aboard!

All Aboard!

fl

th

ch

dr

All Aboard!

Directions for Play
(for 2 Players)

1. Each player chooses one side of the game board.

2. One player shuffles the cards, deals four cards to each player, and places the remaining cards facedown in a pile.

3. The first player spins the spinner and lands on a blend or a digraph. The player looks at his or her cards for a word that begins with the same letters. If the player has such a card, the player places the card in the window labeled with those letters and the turn ends. A player places cards only on his or her side of the board.

4. If the player does not have such a card, he or she takes the top card from the pile. If that card has a word that begins with the same letters, the player places the card in the appropriate window. Otherwise, the player keeps the card.

5. Players continue to take turns. Players may place only one card in each window. If a player lands on the same blend or digraph twice, the player does not place another card and does not choose a card.

6. The first player to fill his or her train wins.

Answer Key

dr	fl	ch	th
dragon	flower	chain	thanks
dream	flag	cheese	think
drum	fluff	chicken	thunder
drink	float	child	Thursday
drain	fly	chimney	thing

All Aboard!

dragon	dream	drum	drink
drain	flower	flag	fluff
float	fly	chain	cheese
chicken	child	chimney	thanks
think	thunder	Thursday	thing

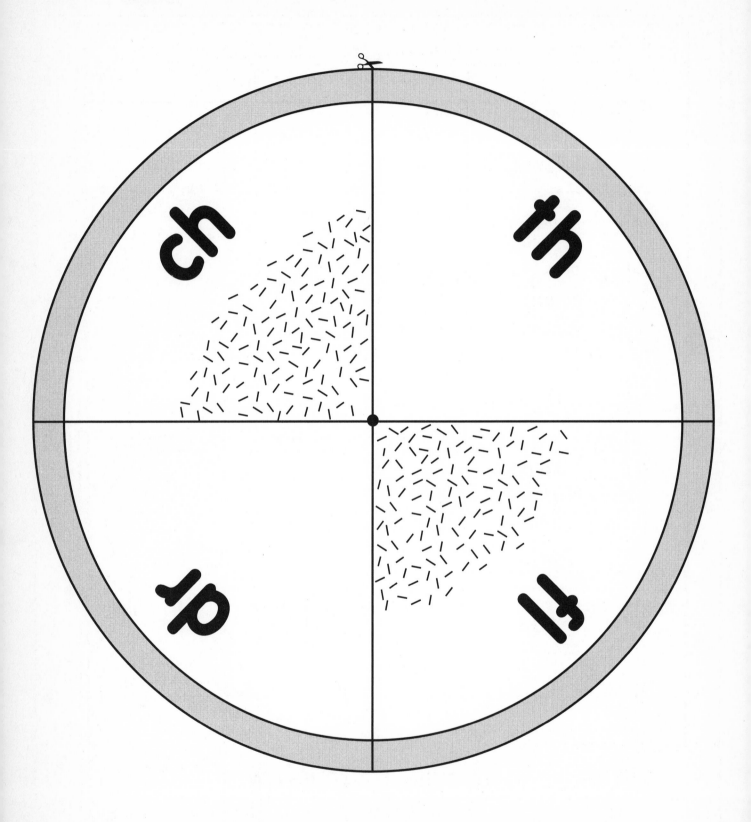

All Aboard!

Game Board

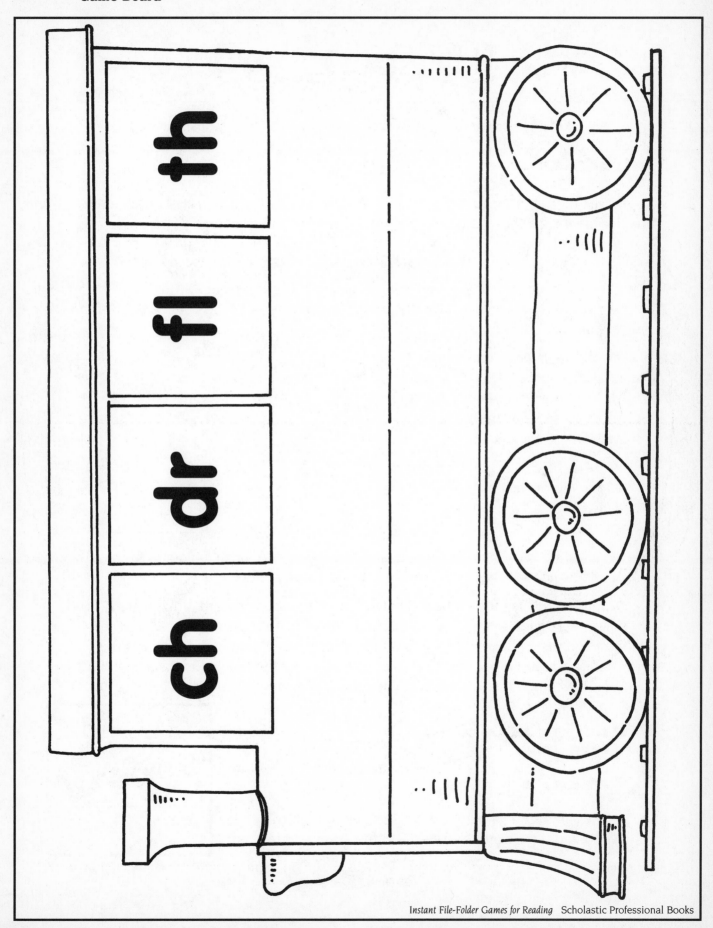

th fl dr ch

Players: 2–3

Bike Race

Skill: This game provides practice in identifying initial consonant sounds.

Introduction

Review the following consonant sounds with children: *s, t, p, f, r, b, n, v.* Allow children to practice identifying these initial consonant sounds in various words.

Assembling the Game

1. Duplicate and cut out the file-folder label and pocket on page 25. Glue the label onto the tab of the file folder. Tape the pocket on three sides to the outside front of the folder.

2. Duplicate and cut out the directions, answer key, and cards on pages 26–27. When the game is not in use, store these items in the pocket on the front of the folder.

3. Make three copies of the playing piece below. Color each playing piece a different color. Fold the tabs so that the pieces stand up.

4. Duplicate and cut out the game board on pages 28–29. Invite students to color the game board, and then glue it onto the inside of the folder.

5. Duplicate the spinner on page 30 and mount it on posterboard or laminate it. To make the spinner, use a large paper clip with either a brass fastener or a pencil. Unbend the end of a paper clip and use it to punch a hole in the center of the spinner. Place the round end of the paper clip over the hole and attach it with a brass fastener. Or spin the paper clip around a pencil tip, as shown on page 18.

Extending the Game

◆ Create additional cards using words that begin with the consonants on the spinner.

◆ Use the cards for a game of concentration in which kids have to find three words that begin with the same letter.

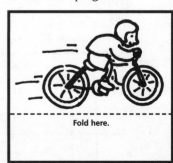

Fold here.

Bike Race

Label and Pocket

Bike Race

Bike Race

Bike Race

Bike Race

Directions for Play
(for 2–3 Players)

1. One player shuffles the cards, deals five cards to each player, and places the remaining cards facedown in a pile.

2. Each player chooses a playing piece and places it on Start.

3. To take a turn, a player spins the spinner. The player reads aloud the letter on which the spinner lands.

4. If the player has a card with a word that begins with that letter, he or she reads aloud that word. The player places the card at the bottom of the pile and moves ahead to the next mile marker.

5. If the player does not have a word that begins with that letter, he or she takes the top card from the pile. If the chosen card has a word that begins with that letter, the player reads aloud the word, places the card at the bottom of the pile, and moves ahead to the next mile marker. If the word does not begin with that letter, the player keeps the card and does not move ahead.

6. Players continue to take turns. The first player to reach mile 10 (the finish line) wins.

Answer Key

b: balloon, basket, button

f: feather, feast, four

n: nickel, napkin, needle

p: pumpkin, pencil, potato

r: rattle, radio, rocket

s: sandwich, sail, seven

t: toothbrush, tomato, telephone

v: valentine, violin, visit

Bike Race

Cards

balloon	basket	button	feather
feast	four	nickel	napkin
needle	pumpkin	pencil	potato
rattle	radio	rocket	sandwich
sail	seven	toothbrush	tomato
telephone	valentine	violin	visit

Bike Race

Game Board

Trim off this strip and attach to page 29.

Bike Race

Game Board

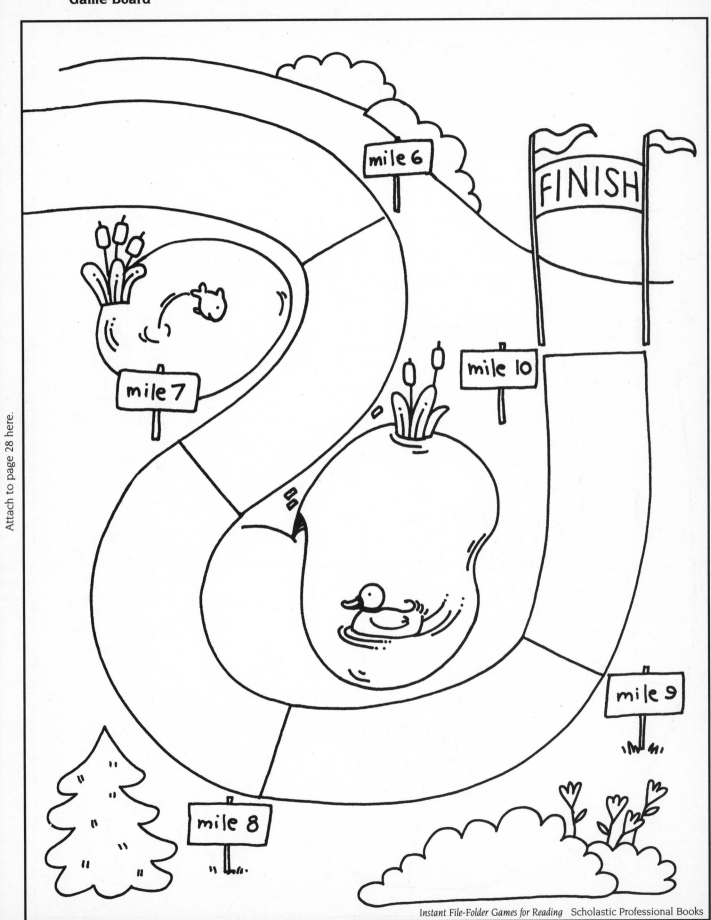

Instant File-Folder Games for Reading   Scholastic Professional Books

Bike Race

Spinner

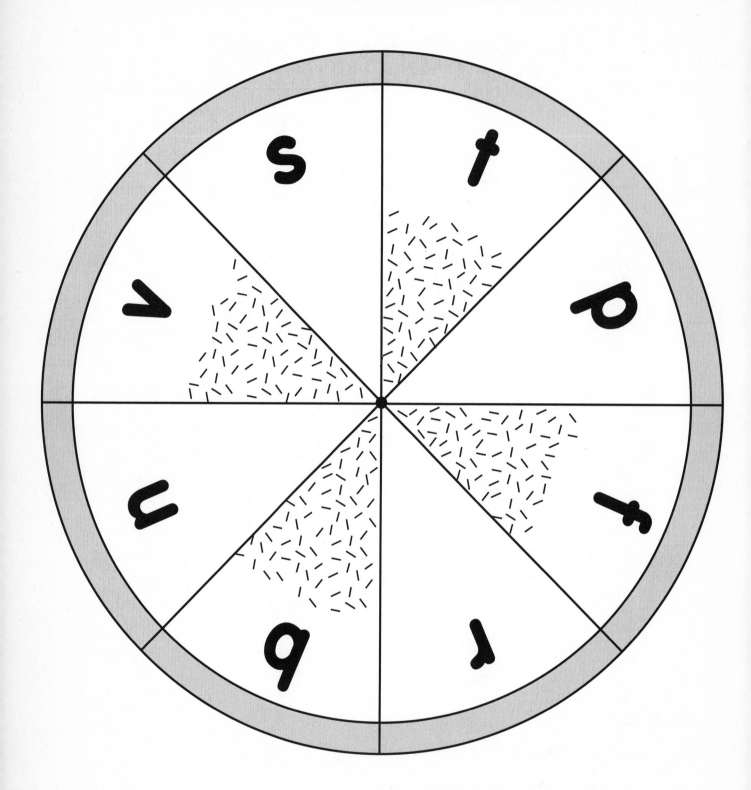

Peas in a Pod

Skill: Children practice matching pairs of synonyms.

Introduction

Review what children know about synonyms. Explain that a synonym is a word that has the same meaning as another word. For example, *large* and *big* are synonyms.

Assembling the Game

1 Duplicate and cut out the file-folder label and pocket on page 32. Glue the label onto the tab of the file folder. Tape the pocket on three sides to the outside front of the folder.

2 Duplicate and cut out the directions, answer key, and cards on pages 33–34. When the game is not in use, store these items in the pocket on the front of the folder.

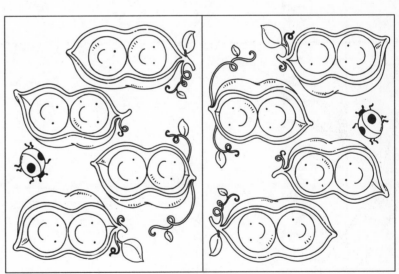

3 Make two copies of the game board on page 35. Invite students to color the game boards, and then glue them onto the inside of the folder.

Extending the Game

✦ Have students use the synonyms in the game in oral or written sentences.

✦ Make additional cards with other synonyms.

Label and Pocket

Peas in a Pod

Peas in a Pod

Peas in a Pod

Directions for Play
(for 2 Players)

✷ Each player chooses one side of the game board.

✷ One player shuffles the cards, deals five cards to each player, and places the remaining cards facedown in a pile. Players do not show their cards to each other.

✷ Each player looks for pairs of synonyms in his or her hand. If a player has a pair (or more than one pair), the player places the two cards in a pod on his or her side of the board.

✷ Player 1 chooses a card from his or her hand. Player 1 reads the word aloud and asks Player 2 if he or she has a synonym.

- If Player 2 has a synonym, Player 2 gives the card to Player 1. Player 1 places the two cards in a pod and the turn ends.

- If Player 2 does not have a synonym, Player 1 chooses the top card from the pile. If Player 1 can make a pair of synonyms, he or she places the cards in a pod and the turn ends. If Player 1 cannot make a pair, he or she keeps the card and the turn ends.

✷ Players continue to take turns. The first player to fill all his or her pods or get rid of all his or her cards wins.

Answer Key

basement, cellar	dirty, filthy	neat, tidy
begin, start	enormous, huge	shop, store
chilly, cold	fast, quick	
correct, right	ill, sick	

Peas in a Pod

quick	fast	shop	store
sick	ill	begin	start
right	correct	basement	cellar
neat	tidy	cold	chilly
dirty	filthy	huge	enormous

Peas in a Pod

Game Board

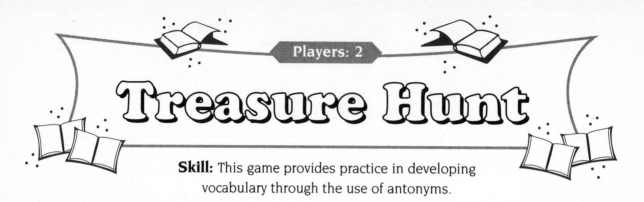

Treasure Hunt

Skill: This game provides practice in developing vocabulary through the use of antonyms.

Introduction
♦♦♦♦♦♦♦♦♦♦♦♦♦♦♦♦♦♦♦

Review what students know about antonyms. Explain that an antonym is a word whose meaning is the opposite of another word. For example, *win* and *lose* are antonyms.

♦♦♦♦♦♦♦♦♦♦♦♦♦♦♦♦♦♦♦♦♦♦ ## Assembling the Game ♦♦♦♦♦♦♦♦♦♦♦♦♦♦♦♦♦♦♦♦♦♦♦♦♦

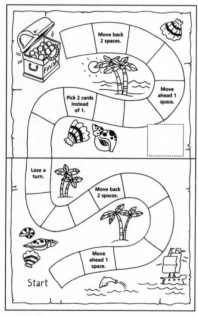

1. Duplicate and cut out the file-folder label and pocket on page 37. Glue the label onto the tab of the file folder. Tape the pocket on three sides to the outside front of the folder.

2. Duplicate and cut out the directions, answer key, and cards on pages 38–39. When the game is not in use, store these items in the pocket on the front of the folder.

3. Duplicate and cut out the number cube below. Fold and glue or tape it together.

4. Duplicate and cut out the game board on pages 40–41. Invite students to color the game board, and then glue it onto the inside of the folder.

NOTE: This game also requires two playing pieces. Dry beans work well.

Extending the Game
♦♦♦♦♦♦♦♦♦♦♦♦♦♦♦♦♦♦♦♦♦♦♦♦♦♦♦♦

♦ Challenge students to use the antonyms in the game in oral or written sentences.

♦ Invite students to think of other antonyms to substitute for the ones on the cards.

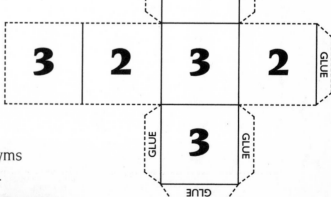

Treasure Hunt

Treasure Hunt

Treasure Hunt

Directions for Play
(for 2 Players)

1 One player shuffles the cards and places them facedown in a pile.

2 Each player chooses a playing piece and places it on Start.

3 The first player rolls the number cube and moves forward that number of spaces. If the space has directions, the player follows them. The player then takes the top card from the pile, reads the word aloud, and tries to think of an antonym. If the player says an antonym, the player keeps the card. If the player does not think of an antonym, the player returns the card to the bottom of the pile. (Note: Players may land on and share the same space.)

4 Players take turns until all players have reached Finish or there are no cards left. (Note: The last player left may need to take several turns in a row.) The player with the most cards wins.

Answer Key

above, below	happy, sad	soft, hard
before, after	hot, cold	tall, short
buy, sell	in, out	top, bottom
clean, dirty	large, small	under, over
down, up	near, far	weak, strong
empty, full	never, always	wet, dry
fast, slow	new, old	win, lose
front, back	same, different	young, old

Treasure Hunt

above	before	buy	clean
down	empty	fast	front
happy	hot	in	large
near	never	new	same
soft	tall	top	under
weak	wet	win	young

Treasure Hunt

Game Board

Cards

Move ahead 1 space.

Move back 2 spaces.

Pick 2 cards instead of 1.

Finish

Treasure Hunt

Game Board

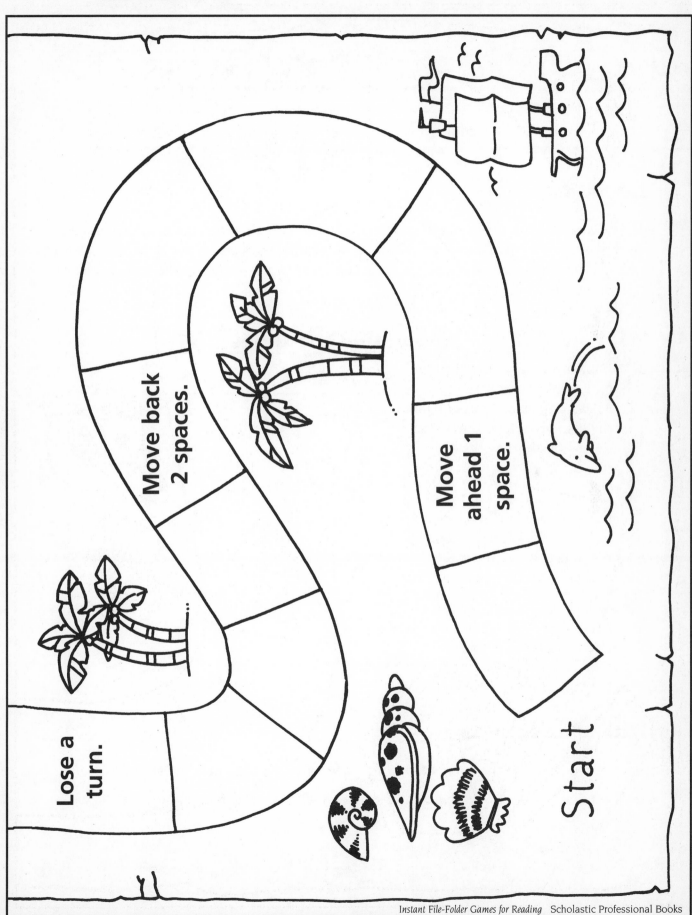

Move back
2 spaces.

Move
ahead 1
space.

Attach to page 40 here.

Lose a
turn.

Start

Word Builders

Skill: This game provides practice in forming
and reading compound words.

Introduction

Review what students know about compound words. Explain that a compound word is a
word that is made up of two or more words. For example, *beanbag* is made up of the words
bean and *bag*. Some compound words are made up of two separate words, such as *fruit fly*,
and others are hyphenated (*send-off*).

Assembling the Game

1. Duplicate and cut out the file-folder label and pocket on page 43. Glue the label onto the tab of the file folder. Tape the pocket on three sides to the outside front of the folder.

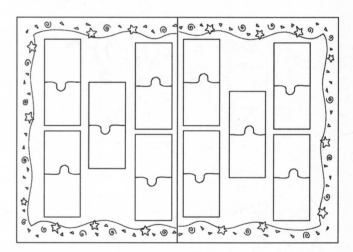

2. Duplicate and cut out the directions, answer key, and cards on pages 44–45. When the game is not in use, store these items in the pocket on the front of the folder.

3. Make two copies of the game board on page 46. Invite students to color the game boards, and then glue them onto the inside of the folder.

Extending the Game

✦ Have students use the compound words they form in oral or written sentences.

✦ As a reading strategy, teach a mini-lesson on taking apart compound words.

Word Builders

Word Builders

book shelf

door

bell

sun flower

Word Builders

Directions for Play
(for 2 Players)

Each player chooses one side of the game board.

Player 1 shuffles the cards, places them facedown beside the game board, and turns over two cards.

Player 2 turns over two more cards. If the player can form a compound word with any of the four cards, he or she places the cards in two connecting puzzle pieces on his or her side of the board. A player can form more than one word per turn. If the player cannot form a word, he or she leaves the cards faceup. (Note: A player turns over only two cards per turn. Players can form words with any cards that are facing up.)

Player 1 turns over two cards. The player tries to form one or more compound words with any cards facing up. If the player can form one or more words, he or she places the cards for each word in connecting puzzle pieces.

Players continue to take turns. The first player to form five compound words on his or her side of the board wins.

Answer Key

Note: You may use a dictionary to look up any words that are not listed here.

anybody	bird dog	doghouse	firelight	playroom	sunlight
anyplace	birdhouse	everybody	fireplace	plaything	sunroom
anything	buttercup	everyplace	fruitcake	somebody	underdog
anywhere	butterfly	everything	fruit fly	someplace	underground
bathhouse	campfire	everywhere	lighthouse	something	
bathroom	campground	firefly	playground	somewhere	
birdbath	cupcake	firehouse	playhouse	sunbath	

Word Builders

sun	bath	cup	cake
fruit	some	place	bird
dog	body	light	butter
room	under	ground	play
camp	fire	fly	house
every	any	where	thing

Word Builders

Game Board

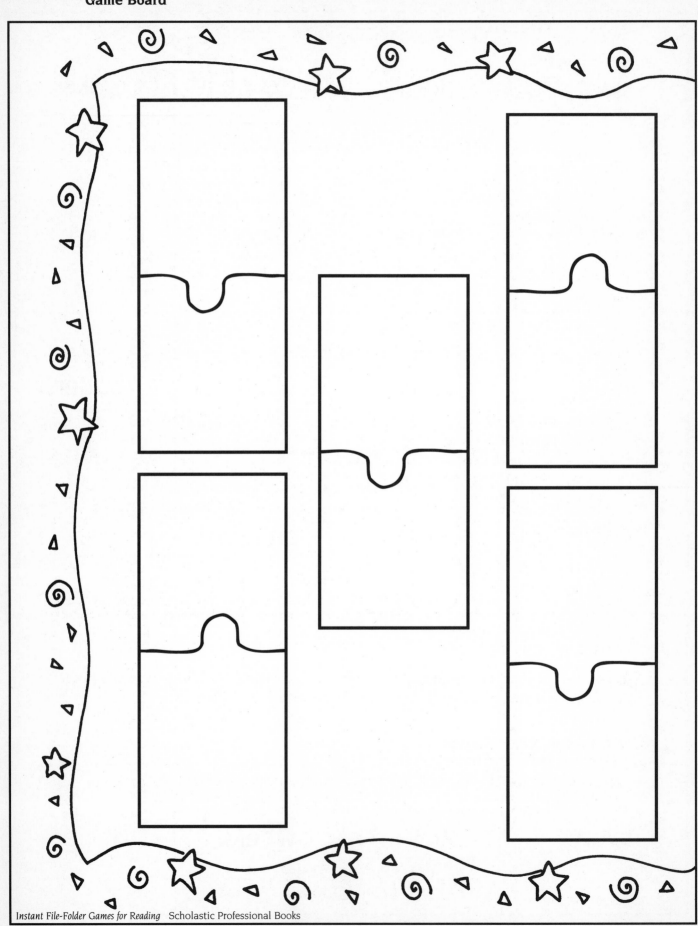

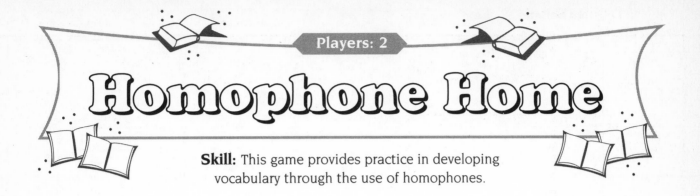

Homophone Home

Skill: This game provides practice in developing vocabulary through the use of homophones.

Introduction
◆◆◆◆◆◆◆◆◆◆◆◆◆◆◆◆◆◆◆◆

Review what students know about homophones. Explain that homophones are words that are pronounced alike but have different meanings and spellings. For example, *male* and *mail* are homophones.

◆◆◆◆◆◆◆◆◆◆◆◆◆◆◆◆◆◆◆◆◆◆◆ **Assembling the Game** ◆◆◆◆◆◆◆◆◆◆◆◆◆◆◆◆◆◆◆◆◆◆◆

1 Duplicate and cut out the file-folder label and pocket on page 48. Glue the label onto the tab of the file folder. Tape the pocket on three sides to the outside front of the folder.

2 Duplicate and cut out the directions, answer key, and cards on pages 49 and 52. When the game is not in use, store these items in the pocket on the front of the folder.

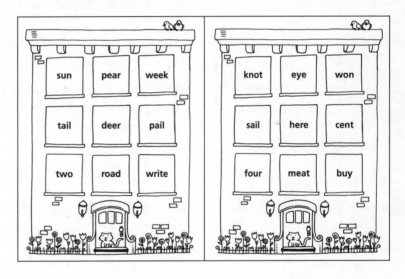

3 Duplicate and cut out game board sides 1 and 2 on pages 50–51. Invite students to color the game board, and then glue it onto the inside of the folder.

Extending the Game
◆◆◆◆◆◆◆◆◆◆◆◆◆◆◆◆◆◆◆◆◆◆◆◆◆

✦ Have students use the homophone pairs in the game in oral or written sentences.

✦ Challenge students to brainstorm other homophone pairs.

Homophone Home

Label and Pocket

Homophone Home

Directions for Play
(for 2 Players)

1 Each player chooses one side of the game board.

2 One player shuffles the cards and places them facedown in a pile.

3 To take a turn, a player picks the top card from the pile and reads the word aloud. If the player has the matching homophone on his or her side of the board, the player places the card facedown on top of the matching homophone and says a sentence with each homophone. If the player does not have the matching homophone, he or she returns the card to the bottom of the pile.

4 Players continue to take turns. The first player to cover three homophones in a row—up, down, or diagonal—wins.

Answer Key

Side 1:

sun, son	road, rode
tail, tale	week, weak
two, too	pail, pale
pear, pair	write, right
deer, dear	

Side 2:

knot, not	meat, meet
sail, sale	won, one
four, for	cent, sent
eye, I	buy, by
here, hear	

Homophone Home

Game Board Side 1

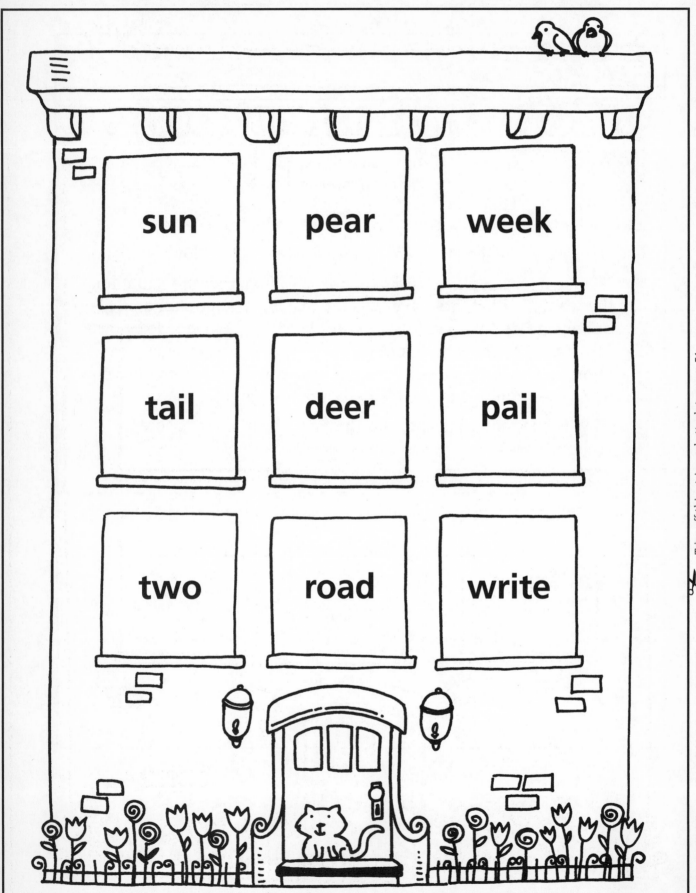

sun	pear	week
tail	deer	pail
two	road	write

Trim off this strip and attach to page 51.

Homophone Home

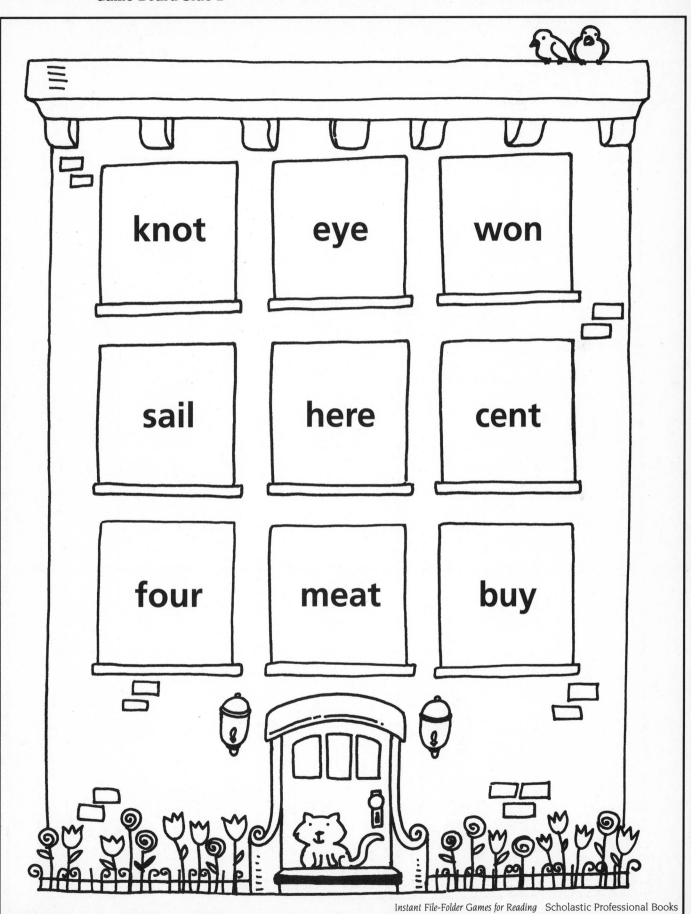

knot   eye   won

sail   here   cent

four   meat   buy

Attach to page 50 here.

Homophone Home

son	tale	too
pair	dear	rode
weak	pale	right
not	sale	for
I	hear	meet
one	sent	by

Word Hop

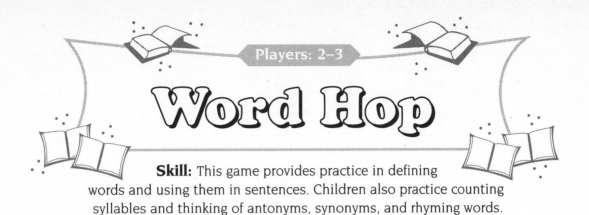

Skill: This game provides practice in defining words and using them in sentences. Children also practice counting syllables and thinking of antonyms, synonyms, and rhyming words.

Introduction

Review antonyms, synonyms, rhyming words, and syllables with children.

Assembling the Game

⭐ 1 Duplicate and cut out the file-folder label and pocket on page 54. Glue the label onto the tab of the file folder. Tape the pocket on three sides to the outside front of the folder.

⭐ 2 Duplicate and cut out the directions, number cube, and cards on pages 55 and 58. When the game is not in use, store these items in the pocket on the front of the folder. Fold and glue or tape together the number cube.

⭐ 3 Make three copies of the playing piece below. Color each playing piece a different color. Fold the tabs so that the pieces stand up.

⭐ 4 Duplicate and cut out the game board on pages 56–57. Invite students to color the game board, and then glue it onto the inside of the folder.

Extending the Game

◆ Teach a mini-lesson on using a dictionary.

◆ Create additional cards for the game so that children can review new vocabulary words.

Fold here.

Word Hop

Word Hop

Word Hop

Directions for Play
(for 2–3 Players)

1 One player shuffles the cards and places them facedown in a pile.

2 Each player chooses a playing piece. Players place their pieces on Start.

3 The first player rolls the number cube and moves forward that number of spaces. The player picks the top card from the pile and reads aloud the word. The player then follows the directions on the space. If the player follows the directions correctly, he or she hops forward one space but does not follow the directions on that space. (Players can use a dictionary or thesaurus to check one another's answers.) If the player does not follow the directions correctly, he or she stays on the same space. The player puts the card at the bottom of the pile.

4 Players continue to take turns. The first player to reach Finish wins.

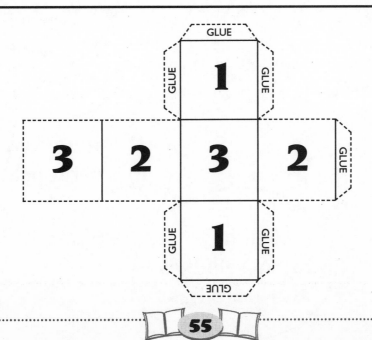

Word Hop

Game Board

Start

Tell how many syllables the word has.

Say another word that begins with the same letter.

Use the word in a sentence.

Tell what the word means.

Tell what the word means.

Think of an antonym, synonym, or rhyming word.

Say another word that begins with the same letter.

Tell how many syllables the word has.

Use the word in a sentence.

Word Hop

Game Board

Think of an antonym, synonym, or rhyming word.

Tell what the word means.

Finish

Tell what the word means.

Tell what the word means.

Use the word in a sentence.

Tell how many syllables the word has.

Use the word in a sentence.

Think of an antonym, synonym, or rhyming word.

Tell what the word means.

Say another word that begins with the same letter.

Word Hop

Cards

strong	agree	chase	float
waste	awake	cheerful	pleasant
gift	noisy	upset	hurry
throw	loose	brag	leave
sour	soak	trail	never
calm	wrong	roam	apart

Join the Parade!

Skill: Children identify nouns and verbs.

Introduction

Explain the difference between nouns and verbs, and provide examples of each. Ask children to brainstorm a list of nouns and verbs.

Assembling the Game

1 Duplicate and cut out the file-folder label and pocket on page 60. Glue the label onto the tab of the file folder. Tape the pocket on three sides to the outside front of the folder.

2 Duplicate and cut out the directions, answer key, and cards on pages 61 and 64. When the game is not in use, store these items in the pocket on the front of the folder.

3 Duplicate and cut out the game board on pages 62–63. Invite students to color the game board, and then glue it onto the inside of the folder.

4 Duplicate and assemble the playing cube below.

Extending the Game

✦ Have children make up sentences using the words on the cards.

✦ Introduce adjectives, and then challenge children to think of words that describe the nouns from the game.

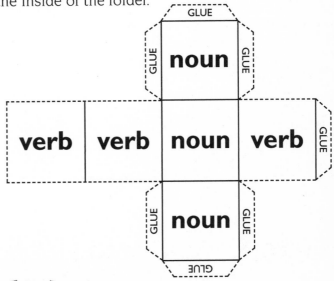

Label and Pocket

Join the Parade!

Join the Parade!

Join the Parade!

Directions for Play
(for 2–4 Players)

⭐**1** One player shuffles the cards and deals them evenly among players. Each player can look at his or her own cards.

⭐**2** The first player rolls the cube. If the player rolls a noun, the player chooses a noun from his or her cards, uses the noun in a sentence, and places the card in the noun pile on the board. If the player rolls a verb, the player chooses a verb, uses the verb in a sentence, and places the card in the verb pile on the board. If a player does not have a card that matches the part of speech, the turn ends.

⭐**3** Players take turns. The first player without any cards left wins.

Answer Key

Nouns:

horn	ice cream
baton	hot dog
drummer	confetti
balloon	butterfly
banner	tree
ears	tail

Verbs:

eat	sing
munch	chew
flutter	listen
celebrate	scatter
relax	see
applaud	enjoy

Join the Parade!

Game Board

Nouns

Join the Parade!

Game Board

Attach to page 62 here.

Verbs

Join the Parade!

Cards

horn	baton	drummer	balloon
banner	ears	ice cream	hot dog
confetti	butterfly	tree	tail
eat	munch	flutter	celebrate
relax	applaud	sing	chew
listen	scatter	see	enjoy